The Netherlands and the United States

A story of old friends

Publication of the Ministry of Foreign Affairs

The Netherlands and the United States, a story of old friends is published by the Foreign Information Service of the Netherlands Ministry of Foreign Affairs. The assistance of Professor A. Lammers of the University of Leiden is gratefully acknowledged.

Author	Koen Sizoo
Editing	Foreign Information Service, Foreign Affairs Information Department
Cover	View of New Amsterdam in 1655, engraving probably dating from 1670, Vingboons Atlas
Design, lithography and graphics	Drukkerij Zuidam & Zonen bv, Woerden
English translation	Translations Department / Liz Berkhof

ISBN 90-74876-11-0

Foreword

The relationship between the Netherlands and the United States of America dates back to the year 1602, when Dutch seafarers en route to Asia landed by mistake in America and discovered a land of undreamed-of potential. This was the beginning of an intensive flow of persons, goods and capital between that great continent and the small, then-powerful maritime state on the North Sea. In various periods, and for various reasons, Dutch people settled in America and contributed to the growth of American society. Traces of them are still discernible not only in the language and in place names, but also in the realms of art, science and politics. Three of America's presidents were descended from Dutch settlers.

Over the years the Dutch and the Americans have each taken note of the other's political and cultural ideas, often with admiration and occasionally with disapproval. Our economic and political relations have nevertheless moved steadily forward without any serious disruption. Among the highlights of this relationship is the Marshall Plan, which was a crucial element in the economic reconstruction of the Netherlands after the Second World War. Fifty years later, we are commemorating this truly exceptional gesture of friendship.

Nearly four hundred years of our relationship are outlined in the following pages. I have great pleasure in presenting this bird's-eye view of a fascinating past, which is also a promise for the future.

Hans van Mierlo
Minister for Foreign Affairs

View of St Eustatius, engraving by K.F. Bensdorp

1.1. Het Boven Dorp
1.2.2. Beneden Dorp
3. de Hollandsche Kerk
4. 't Oude Padt
5. 't Nieuwe Padt

6. 't Fort Oranje
7. de Vlaag en Landing-Plaat voor 't Oude Padt
8. Landing-Plaat voor 't Nieuwe Padt

GEZIGT VAN HET EYLAND
St. EUSTATIUS.
Den Wel Eerwaardigen Heere CONRADUS SCHWIERS J.J.Th.Dr. en Gewezen Predikant
word deeze Plaat Opgedraagen, door zyn Wel. Eerw. D.W. Dienaar
G.J. van Paddenburg

Introduction

On November 16, 1776, cannon boomed out at St. Eustatius, an island of the Antilles group in the West Indies. In the roads off the island, an outpost of the Dutch colonial empire, lay a small two-master flying a flag which had only recently appeared on the world's seas. Its thirteen red and white stripes symbolized the thirteen states that some four months earlier had united in the Continental Congress and declared their independence from the British Crown.

As was customary for ships entering a foreign port, Captain Josiah Robinson of the Andrew Doria had ordered a salute to be fired. The commander of the shore fort hesitated to respond, for no-one had yet recognized the new state. The governor of the island, Johannes de Graaff, then ordered him to fire the return salute. The guns of Fort Orange roared, and for the first time in history the American flag was saluted by an official representative of another power. The famous first salute at St. Eustatius marked the beginning of international recognition of the new nation. It was also the beginning of its official relations with the Netherlands. The fact that the Dutch Republic was the first to salute the American flag was however no coincidence. Close ties had long existed between the North American colonies and the Republic of the United Provinces. In the centuries before, the Republic had played a prominent part in the discovery, colonization and population of the region. And in the years that followed the Dutch were to be no less involved with the fortunes of the state they had just welcomed into the community of nations.

A pinnace (warship) by C. Verbeek, c. 1625

New Netherland

1

The Netherlands' contacts with the New World dated back to the first half of the sixteenth century, well before the emergence of the Republic on the North Sea. The Low Countries, one of the most densely populated regions in Europe, were not a unitary state but an agglomeration of seventeen separate small provinces under the Spanish Crown. As subjects of the king of Spain, Dutch merchants had ready access to other parts of the Spanish Empire, including the Americas. Even after 1568, when the northern provinces rose in revolt against Philip II, that remained largely unchanged.

In 1581 the seven northern provinces proclaimed their independence from Spain with the Act of Abjuration (Plakkaat van Verlatinge), a solemn declaration that the king could no longer be acknowledged as their sovereign lord because of his "acts of tyranny". A highly revolutionary act in those days,

it shook the thrones of Europe and set a precedent which was subsequently followed by others. Nearly two centuries later, the same concept was applied in respect of the British Crown, forming the bedrock of the American Declaration of Independence.

It was eighty years before Spain finally acknowledged the independence of the Netherlands. The young nation, a loosely federated republic whose seven provinces each possessed a large measure of autonomy, evolved in those years into one of the most powerful states in Europe. Amsterdam became a center of world trade, dealing in timber and grain from the Baltic, salt from the French Atlantic coast, Portugal and the West Indies, spices from the Far East and furs from North America, and occupying a central position in the arms trade, the capital market and the provision of financial services. In 1580

The Halve Maen (replica)

Hudson rounded Cape Cod and entered Long Island Sound in search of a northwest passage to the Pacific. On September 12 he sighted "as fine a river as can be found, wide and deep, with good anchoring on both sides."

its population was 30,000 to 40,000; over the next hundred years it grew to more than 200,000.

The Golden Age, as this period of Dutch history is known, owed much of its prosperity to the Republic's vast commercial empire that stretched from the Indian Ocean to the Hudson River. Most of its mercantile activities were concentrated in the hands of trading companies granted a monopoly of seaborne trade by the States General, the assembly of provincial delegates which constituted the central government. The largest such company, the Dutch East India Company (VOC), was founded in 1602 to trade with the Far East. Its governing body, the Heeren XVII, constantly seeking to reduce costs, made repeated attempts to find a northern passage to the Orient to replace the hazardous route round the Cape of Good Hope.

After several failed expeditions, often with heavy loss of life and ships, the small seventy-ton Halve Maen set sail in April 1609 with a ship's company of sixteen commanded by the English navigator Henry Hudson. He first set course for the northeast,

but before reaching Novaya Zemlya was forced by the Arctic ice to put about. Having survived a near mutiny, the loss of his mast in a storm and a skirmish with Indians on the Newfoundland coast, Hudson at length reached the North Atlantic coast of the New World.

The English, founders in 1607 of Jamestown in Virginia, had laid claim to all land, known and unknown, to the north of Jamestown, but had never backed this grandiose claim with maps. Prior to the voyage of the Halve Maen, Dutch fishing vessels had penetrated to the region south of the 44th parallel (running just to the north of Portland, Maine), but that stretch of coast was still largely unexplored. Hudson rounded Cape Cod and entered Long Island Sound in search of a northwest passage to the Pacific. On September 12 he sighted "as fine a river as can be found, wide and deep, with good anchoring on both sides," and leading moreover in a northerly direction. Ninety miles upstream he was forced to conclude that it was not the hoped-for northwest passage. The river grew ever shallower and the crew

were again on the verge of mutiny. Deeply disappointed, Hudson had to end his quest, unaware of the fact that in exploring this waterway he had sailed into history.

The voyage having failed in its principal aim, the directors of the Dutch East India Company, who had sponsored the expedition, showed little interest in Hudson's discoveries. Others were more alert. Soon afterwards accounts of the voyage appeared, portraying the newly discovered territory as a true paradise. Johannes de Laet, author of The New World or a Description of the West Indies, a popular series of travelers' tales, described this new land as "pleasant and fertile", well suited to habitation, with a mild climate and abundant crops which grew virtually by themselves. This was music to the ears of Dutch merchants, who lost no time in fitting out ships for the voyage to "Hudson's river". Those who set off after reading these tales of De Laet

One of the first detailed maps of the east coast of North America, based on information gathered by Captain Adriaen Block, 1614

(and of others who painted a still rosier picture: some even endowed the region with a tropical climate) were unpleasantly surprised when they encountered the severe winters of North America. Nevertheless, for some merchants the voyages were profitable enough to warrant their continuation.

Merchantmen left Amsterdam carrying firearms, alcohol, textiles and all manner of trinkets to trade with the Indians for skins and beaver pelts. Noting the success of the first ventures, more merchants rushed to trade with North America. As greater competition drove up the prices offered for their pelts, this might seem to have been to the advantage of the Amerindian population. Instead, the tribes living along the banks of the Hudson then began to compete with each other in their dealings with the Europeans, which led to strife. Now that they possessed firearms, friction between them often ended in bloodshed. Furthermore, they grew increasingly dependent on the alcohol, gunpowder and shot which only the Europeans could supply. The situation was explosive in more than one respect.

In Amsterdam, the merchants were becoming worried, for competition lowered the profits and heightened the risks. But as it happened, they had more to fear from one another than from the Indians. The storm broke in 1613. In the autumn of that year the Fortuyn, the Nachtegael and the Tijger lay at anchor in the mouth of the Hudson. The three captains were locked in fierce competition for the pelts brought by the Indians, each outbidding the other and driving up the price day after day. All attempts to reach agreement failed. With the onset of winter they were still there, and their holds were still empty. A disastrous fire which destroyed the Tijger down to the waterline (parts of the wreck were recovered in 1916 on the present-day site of the WTC's Twin Towers) caused the final eruption.

While Captain Adriaen Block was ashore directing the building of a new ship, his crew mutinied, seized the Nachtegael, set ashore her captain, Thijs Mossel, and his few loyal crew members and sailed away. The sole remaining seaworthy ship, the

Fortuyn, commanded by Hendrik Christiaensen, was too small to carry more than her own complement over the Atlantic. For Block, Mossel and their men the outlook was bleak. But even that did not end their quarreling, Mossel now going so far as to accuse Block of having incited his crew to mutiny.

The competitiveness which had caused this débâcle proved however to have a positive side as well. The stranded mariners were rescued from their perilous situation by two newly arrived ships, the Vos out of Amsterdam, and a second Fortuyn, out of Hoorn. Good Samaritans they may have been, ready and willing to save their unfortunate compatriots, but the matter of costs was not forgotten. In return for half their stock of furs the castaways could be taken aboard for the homeward voyage. It was an offer they could not refuse. The two Fortuyns and the Vos, all carrying a full cargo of furs, returned to Holland in July 1614.

The merchants in Amsterdam decided that something must be done to prevent this sort of thing happening again. In 1615 a group of them obtained from the States General a monopoly of the Hudson trade. Their charter was the first document in which the name New Netherland appeared. Though it existed for just three years, the New Netherland Company was reasonably successful. A number of trading posts were established, and ships departed regularly both to trade and to chart the coastal waters. The eastern seaboard from Connecticut to the Carolinas was charted in this way by cartographers in the service of the Company.

In 1618 an application for a renewal of the charter, which this time was also to encompass the lands around the mouth of the Delaware River, was refused by the States General for internal political reasons. Notwithstanding this loss of their official monopoly, the former members of the Company experienced little difficulty in continuing their trade with New Netherland. For only they possessed the experience, the contacts and the funds essential to the success of such hazardous ventures.

Coins of the Golden Age: Spanish pieces of eight

West Indies House in Amsterdam (headquarters of the West India Company)

In 1621 the States General established the West India Company, modeled on the extremely successful VOC. The Dutch merchants were enthusiastic. During a twelve-year truce with Spain, which was about to expire, the Republic had greatly prospered. Although this prosperity was partly due to the fact that capital and manpower had not been expended on warfare, some were convinced that a resumption of hostilities would bring even greater rewards because war would give the Republic the opportunity to seize the rich Spanish colonies in the New World. It was no coincidence that the WIC appeared on the scene just as the twelve-year truce was coming to an end, not the least of the considerations being the new Company's potential as a weapon. The overly optimistic view of its own strength prevailing in the Republic at that time was reflected in the Company's articles of association, which claimed a monopoly of all trade throughout the whole of the Western Hemisphere.

At first the WIC focused more on privateering in the waters of the Spanish Americas, which promised to be more lucrative in the short term, than on trade and colonization. Some of its successes were indeed spectacular. Admiral Piet Heyn became a legendary figure in Dutch history after his capture in 1628 of a Spanish silver fleet worth some twelve million guilders off the coast of Cuba. Fitting out the privateers however involved huge costs - Piet Heyn's expedition cost the WIC approximately five million guilders - which on the whole were not offset by their successes. By the end of the first ten years of its operations the Company found itself in lasting financial difficulties.

From Sinterklaas to Santa Claus

St Nicholas's annual arrival in Amsterdam

Many Americans would probably be highly surprised to learn that Santa Claus, or Father Christmas, doesn't come from the North Pole at all, but from the Netherlands. The "birthday" of Sinterklaas, or Saint Nicholas, has been celebrated in the Netherlands for centuries. A fourth-century bishop of Myra, in present-day Turkey, he was the patron saint of seafarers, of the city of Amsterdam, and of children. Through the years the feast of St. Nicholas, traditionally held on the evening of December 5th, has become a colorful mixture of time-honored and modern folklore.

A few weeks before the big day Sinterklaas, mounted on his white horse and accompanied by a retinue of Moorish servants, arrives by steamboat "from Spain," where he is assumed to live. This fiction simply underscores the fact that he lives "far away," like his American counterpart; there is no connection between Spain and the historical figure of St. Nicholas. The saintly visitor, wearing a long white beard and the robes of a medieval bishop, is welcomed by civic dignitaries and crowds of children. His arrival is broadcast live on television.

Then Sinterklaas starts on his annual task of distributing presents. He consults his Great Book to see who deserve presents for being good children in the past year. Those who were naughty risk being chastised by his servant Black Peter, or worse, being taken off to Spain to learn to behave. So in these three weeks Dutch children live between hope and fear. At bedtime they place a shoe by the hearth (with a carrot or sugar lumps for Sinterklaas's horse to win his good opinion) in the hope of finding a present in it next morning. Mounted on his wonderful white horse, he rides at night over the rooftops and drops presents down the chimneys with the help of his servants. In the morning the children usually find their shoes contain a small toy or some of the sweets traditionally distributed at Sinterklaas parties in schools, etc. On the evening of December 5th the members of the family give presents to one another, all of which of course "have been left by Sinterklaas." Each present, which is accompanied by a poem addressed to the recipient, is elaborately packaged. For practical jokers who enjoy seeing others up to their elbows in syrup and sawdust this is the highlight of the year.

Dutch children long retain their belief in Sinterklaas. For three weeks every year the Netherlands is in the grip of an adult conspiracy not to shatter the illusion. Many people will say that one of the worst moments of their childhood was the discovery that Sinterklaas didn't exist after all.

Babel on the Hudson

2

Meanwhile, with the Company's blessing, the Hudson fur trade was largely in the hands of private enterprise. But when its other activities proved to be considerably less profitable than originally envisaged, the WIC began to take a more active interest in the fur trade. This was not at all to the colonists' liking. In fact the settlement did not really begin to prosper until the Company, constantly under threat of bankruptcy (to which it finally succumbed in 1674), was no longer capable of running the colony.

That is not to say that the role of the WIC was insignificant. It was responsible, for instance, for the settlement of the first European colonists in New Netherland, spurred on by the covetous looks cast at the territory by France and Britain. The directors of the WIC realized that the only way to strengthen their position in the New World was to encourage permanent settlement. Thirty Walloon families, refugees from the part of the Netherlands still under Spanish rule, set out for America in 1624. They were put ashore in small groups at the mouth of the Delaware, the Hudson and the Connecticut rivers, marking the extent of the territory claimed by the Dutch. The most northerly outpost was established on the upper reaches of the Hudson, just south of present-day Albany. Its wooden blockhouse was named Fort Orange after William of Orange, who had led the Netherlands to independence and whose family were the hereditary stadholders, the heads of state of the Republic.

The Walloon families were not the first to leave the Low Countries to build a new life in America. Four years earlier a group of English refugees, religious dissidents who were opposed to the king and the Anglican

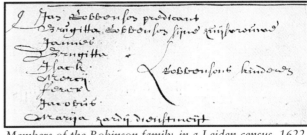
Members of the Robinson family, in a Leiden census, 1622

The Pilgrim Fathers in the Netherlands

The odyssey of the English religious dissidents known as the Pilgrim Fathers began in 1608, when they left their homes near Scrooby in the North Midlands to escape persecution in the reign of King James I. Led by John Robinson, a former Fellow of Corpus Christi College, Cambridge, these Nonconformists crossed the North Sea in the hope of practicing their religion without hindrance in Holland. Complete freedom of religion did not exist anywhere in Europe at that time, but those who professed unorthodox beliefs were generally left alone in the Republic.

First they settled in Amsterdam, but became embroiled in a religious conflict with other English exiles and moved a year later to Leiden, one of the Republic's most important and prosperous centers, "a fair and bewtifull citie." King James instructed his ambassador to make life difficult for his Nonconformist subjects, but the city fathers of Leiden gave them protection and allowed them to settle. They were to live there for the next 11 years; some, like John Robinson, stayed for the rest of their lives. Their number grew to about 135, and they gradually became integrated into Dutch life. Many worked as laborers in the cloth industry. The Elders - Robinson, William

Brewster and Thomas Brewer - held posts at the University of Leiden. They conducted their services in Robinson's house in De Groene Poort (The Green Close) in the Kloksteeg. Brewster and Brewer set up a printing house in Pieterskerkchoorsteeg (St. Peter's Church Choir Alley), a street still in existence today, where they printed religious books and pamphlets for distribution in England. Highly incensed, the English authorities exerted heavy diplomatic pressure on the Dutch to close down the Pilgrim Press.

There was some intermarriage with the local community, and even though the Pilgrims were joined by a number of converts like Philippe De la Noye, an ancestor of Franklin Delano Roosevelt, Robinson feared the group would eventually be assimilated into

the Dutch community, so encouraged their departure for the New World. Their first idea was to emigrate to New Netherland, but the States General, finding it inexpedient to provoke England at that moment, refused permission. The Pilgrims then sought contact with an English company and were granted a charter to found a colony in New England. John Robinson stayed in Leiden, where he died in 1625.

The emigrants, amongst whom were only a few of the first Pilgrims who had arrived from England, left Leiden in July 1620. Traveling by canal boat to Delfshaven, a port near Rotterdam, they boarded the Speedwell to cross the Atlantic, but the ship was not robust enough for such a voyage. In Southampton they transferred to the Mayflower.

Unveiling of a wall tablet - probably in 1906 - in the Jean Pesijnhof in Leiden to commemorate John Robinson's stay there

Church, had sought permission to settle in New Netherland. Their request was refused. The States General had no wish to provoke the English at the very moment when the war with Spain was about to be resumed. But the Pilgrims were not to be deterred. Returning to England, they set sail for America in the Mayflower, landing in 1620 as the vanguard of the stream of immigrants who were to colonize New England.

View of Leiden in the 17th century, engraving by Visscher de Lange

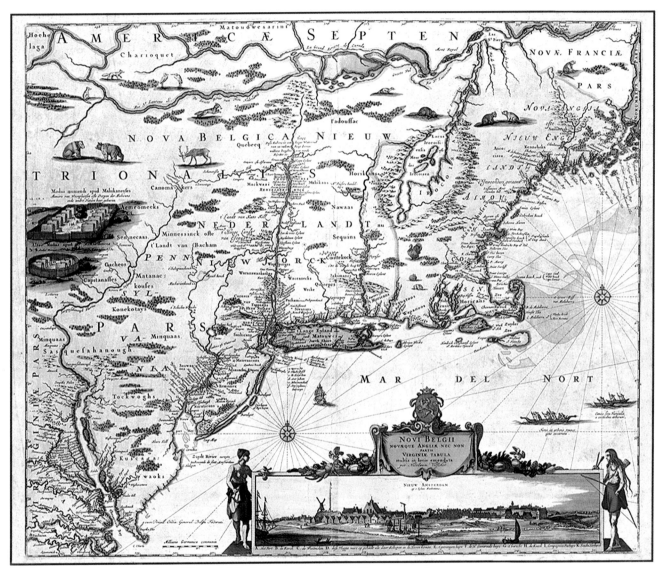

Map of New Netherland by Jansz-Visser, 1682. Lower right: view of New Amsterdam

The Pilgrims were made welcome by the local people, but did not wish to be integrated into Dutch society, which at that time was absorbing many newcomers from all over Europe. In the New World they hoped to avoid such a cultural melting-pot and to retain their own identity.

The Pilgrim Fathers, as they came to be known in American history, lived twelve years in the Republic, the majority of them in and around Amsterdam, Leiden and Rotterdam. They were made welcome by the local people, but did not wish to be integrated into Dutch society, which at that time was absorbing many newcomers from all over Europe. In the New World they hoped to avoid such a cultural melting pot and to retain their own identity.

Four years after the Pilgrims' request, the Dutch were less cautious about provoking English ire. As Britain had no intention of relinquishing her claims to New Netherland, it was considered essential to establish a colony in assertion of their rights to the territory. An additional reason may have been the fact that Walloons were not well liked in the Republic, even though they were persecuted by the Spanish for the Calvinist beliefs they shared with the Dutch. They had the reputation of being argumentative.

The WIC took its time in organizing its American colony. Before leaving, the colonists had to sign a document pledging obedience to the Company's rules during the voyage and after their arrival. The Company determined where they would live and what crops they were to grow. The colony was headed by a director general, or governor, appointed by the Company. The laws, the administration of justice and the official religion had to be those of the mother country.

These rules, which were set out in what were called the Provisional Orders, were less strict in practice than they first seemed. To be sure, the governor was the highest authority in the colony, but he was obliged to accept the assistance of a council representing the colonists. The rule that the settlers must adhere to the rigid Calvinist doctrine of the Synod of Dordrecht was presumably intended to reassure those at home; in actual fact the Company did not interfere with people's religious convictions, and it was years before the first official minister was sent to New Netherland. The land allocated to the colonists varied according to the size of each family. The governor decided what crops they were to grow. On the other hand, besides the land, their passage was free and the Company undertook to supply livestock on interest-free credit at "a fair price." They were also encouraged to engage in the fur trade and to search for minerals. The idea behind all this was that the Dutch claim to the territory was in large part dependent on the success of the colony, and this being the case, the Company did all it could to ensure its success by providing the colonists with the necessary resources, freedom and protection.

A year after the arrival of the first thirty families, a convoy of six ships left Amsterdam for New Netherland, carrying food supplies, weapons, agricultural tools, seeds, livestock and several hundred new settlers. Despite the thorough preparations made by the Company, before long the survival of the colony was hanging by a thread. Dispersing the settlers over different locations proved to have been a mistake. It was difficult to supply the settlers on the coast, and the fortresses at the river mouths could not be defended against attack from the hinterland. The Indian tribes around Fort Orange were at war with one another, bringing the fur trade to

a virtual standstill. And finally, they were threatening to attack the white intruders who had usurped their land.

In the spring of 1626 Governor Pieter Minuit decided to relocate all the colonists on the centrally situated island of Manhattan, which was easier to defend. Conditions were primitive at first: the families lived in dug-out huts or shared the stalls with their livestock. The building of a fort and houses got under way after the island was purchased from the Indians for 60 guilders, a bargain even for those times. That sum today would not buy even a square meter of land on Manhattan.

The settlement that arose before the winter was named Fort New Amsterdam. It comprised thirty wooden houses, a simple fort, a stone weigh-house and a mill whose loft doubled as a church. The colonists immediately embarked on trading activities with such enthusiasm that Minuit had to warn them not to neglect other essential things like growing food. Even so, the new colony did not yield the WIC the profits it had anticipated. That was

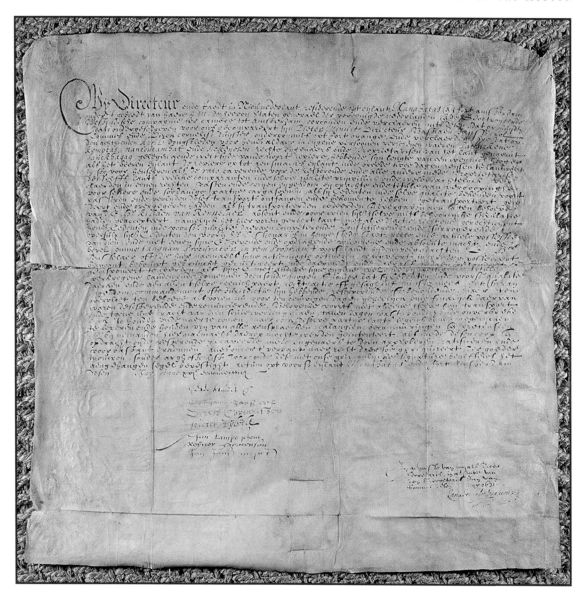

Certificate of purchase of land in what is now Albany, New York, signed by P. Minuit, 1631

partly because the colonists were not experienced traders, but also because prices went up and smuggling was widespread. The directors, the Heeren XIX, soon lost interest and left the further conduct of affairs to a number of Amsterdam merchants who saw potential in the enterprise.

In 1628, in an effort to attract more immigrants and make New Netherland more economically viable, the merchants devised a near-feudal system of large-scale farming - known as "patroonship" - based on large estates. The "patroon" was granted ownership of a large holding in return for financing the settlement of fifty immigrants over the next four years. The Freedoms and Exemptions, the rules governing the patroonships, endowed the landowner with unlimited power over his workers, even the power to pass sentence of death.

A number of such estates came into being along the Hudson and at the mouth of the Delaware, but they were not a great success. Other Amsterdam merchants worked against the new colonial landowners, and Swanendael, an estate on the Delaware, was overrun by Indians. One by one the patroons left their estates. After 1636 only the Van Rensselaers, owners of Rensselaerswijck on the Hudson, still remained. As great landowners they continued to play a leading part in the affairs of the colony long after it had passed into English hands.

The experiment with large-scale agriculture as the overarching system having failed, the colony returned to smaller-scale activities. The colonists grew various European crops, primarily cereals (wheat, barley, oats), kept horses, cows, pigs and poultry, and cultivated tobacco for export to Europe. They traded extensively with the Indians living further inland for the much sought-after beaver and otter pelts, which were so prized - with hard currency in such short supply - that they were sometimes used in lieu of money. Doctor Hans Kierstede, whose house on the Marktvelt stood where Pearl Street now joins Whitehall Street, once dressed a stab wound "against payment of one beaver." The principal activity in New Netherland remained the trade in otter and beaver pelts, a vastly rewarding source of income

The Republic at that time was probably the most powerful state in Europe; it was certainly the most prosperous. It held a strong attraction for foreigners seeking a better life.

which kept the colony going but at the same time impeded further development. There was no need to look for other means of subsistence. Furthermore, as the fur trade was wholly in the hands of merchants in Amsterdam, there was no separate class of influential merchants in the colony, as was the case in New England. New Amsterdam was still bound by many ties to the mother country. Illustrative in this respect is the fact that supplies for the colonists were the second most lucrative trade for the Amsterdam merchants in New Netherland.

Notwithstanding the narrow economic base, the population of the colony steadily increased, though its growth rate was in no way comparable to that of neighboring New England, where streams of immigrants were arriving. In 1643 the population numbered between 400 and 500; by 1654 it had increased a good five-fold to 2600, and ten years later had more than tripled again to 9000.

The Republic at that time was probably the most powerful state in Europe; it was certainly the most prosperous. It held a strong attraction for foreigners seeking a better life. Via the Republic many found their way to the Dutch colonies, where they hoped to make their fortunes. New Netherland was just one of the possible choices: they could equally well try their luck in the East Indies or Brazil, or sign on as a sailor aboard a VOC ship. The same opportunities were available to Dutchmen unable to find work at home. There were no specific groups, like the English Puritans, who for religious or other reasons emigrated together to the colonies.

Consequently, the population of New Netherland increased much less rapidly and was also much less homogeneous than in the English colonies. Many of the immigrants - half of them, according to some estimates - were not from the mother country. Roughly 19 percent came from Germany, and 15 percent from England, while others were from Norway, Sweden, Denmark, Finland and France. The French priest Isaac Jogues, visiting New Amsterdam in 1643, heard as many as eighteen different languages spoken, though

NIEUW AMSTERDAM OFTE NUE NIEUW IORX OPT TEYLANT MAN

View of New Amsterdam in 1655, engraving probably dating from 1670, Vingboons Atlas

there were only about 500 people there at that time. In his judgement the settlement had "the arrogance of Babel."

As distinct from the surrounding English colonies, the population was not exclusively European. Early on, the WIC had brought African slaves to

The French priest Isaac Jogues, visiting New Amsterdam in 1643, heard as many as eighteen different languages spoken, though there were only about 500 people there at that time. In his judgement the settlement had "the arrogance of Babel."

the colony to work in the port, but in the absence of a plantation economy there was no demand for large numbers of slaves. Round 1660 they comprised some 5 percent of the population. New Amsterdam however functioned as a slave market for the British colonies in the south.

After years of faithful service, the Company slaves could win a substantial measure of freedom of movement and property rights on condition that they paid the Company a certain sum of money each year. Many slaves were ultimately freed by their masters, and were assigned a plot of land by the Company. Even those who were not free had some civil rights, such as the right to marry in both civil and church ceremonies. The Dutch trusted their slaves, as is clear from plans to arm teams of slaves for guerrilla operations during the Indian Wars of 1641 and 1660.

The Indians and the Dutch were at first on friendly terms. Unlike the colonists in neighboring New England, the Swannekens (people from the sea), as they were called by the indigenous inhabitants, were not driven by fanatical hatred of "the heathen

savages" to try to wipe them out. They traded with the surrounding Indians and adopted some aspects of their culture, such as the cultivation of maize - the only cereal that could be grown on a large scale in the region - the extraction of maple sugar, and certain medicinal remedies. The WIC had impressed on the settlers that friendly relations with the indigenous population would be in the interests of peace. This rule was more or less followed in the early years. An Indian with a grievance against a colonist could apply to the court in New Amsterdam for redress, and it happened more than once that such a complaint was upheld.

Just the same, in New Netherland as elsewhere Indians were not regarded as true equals. They were forbidden to ride horses, were paid less than whites for the same work, and were often denied payment of money they had earned. The sale of alcohol and firearms to Indians was prohibited, but there were many Dutch traders who yielded to the temptation to supply them with these commodities in exchange for beaver pelts. The Indians grew steadily more resentful of official discrimination and opposition. There had been some skirmishes in the past, but they paled in comparison with the wars which erupted in the colony from 1640 onward. The casus belli was an announcement by Governor Kieft that his indigenous "subjects" would henceforth be required to pay taxes. It triggered a number of extremely violent confrontations between the "Swannekens" and the "Savages" in the years from 1640 to 1664 which inflicted enormous damage on both sides. The most striking consequences, and the most serious, were the depopulation of vast areas for many years and the erosion of confidence in the future of the colony, which lost its attraction for potential immigrants while the surrounding English settlements were growing apace.

While New Amsterdam was never anywhere near the size of its namesake in Europe, it had one characteristic in common with the older town: it too was a bustling, cosmopolitan port frequented by many nationalities. Because of its commercial focus, foreigners were constantly coming and going. More than any other North American colony, New Amsterdam was a melting pot almost from the start, as exemplified by one of the entries in the town's marriage register, recording the marriage of a European to an African woman, presumably a freed slave.

Social life combined the characteristics of a frontier town and a trade center. The tolerance for which the Dutch were renowned, stemming in part from the idea that it was foolish to give offence to anyone who might turn out to be useful, resulted in a proliferation of taverns and brothels. On his arrival in 1647, the Reverend Backerus was horrified to find seventeen or more taverns where his flock could slake their thirst. Whereas it was years before a church was built - the loft of the old mill still served that purpose - an official municipal inn was one of the first stone buildings to arise, standing on the spot where Pearl Street now intersects Coenties Alley (named after the shoemaker Coenraedt Ten Eyck, whose workshop stood there). Excavations on the site in 1979 unearthed large quantities of Dutch pottery.

Life in New Amsterdam was often

On one occasion the residents were treated to the spectacle of their inebriated spiritual leader being chased down the street by their equally inebriated governor, sword in hand. Needless to say, the Company's directors could not condone such behavior, and both were eventually recalled.

riotous and disorderly. Within three months, the first landlord of the inn, Philip Gerritsen, was stabbed to death in a quarrel with a customer. Drunken brawls were commonplace, and almost everyone around joined in the fray. Backerus's predecessor, Everardus Bogardus (it was usual for clergymen's names to be latinized), had a reputation for looking for trouble with other dignitaries when in his cups. Wouter van Twiller, the third governor of the colony, was likewise known for his attachment to the gin bottle, which did not enhance his decision-making and executive capacities. On one occasion the residents were treated to the spectacle of their inebriated spiritual leader being chased down the street by their equally inebriated governor, sword in hand. Needless to say, the Company's directors could not condone such behavior, and both were eventually recalled. Their successors, Kieft and Backerus, and later Stuyvesant, waged an unceasing battle against the intemperance of the colonists, though with little success.

In May 1647 the man arrived who was to be identified more than any

other with New Amsterdam, and ultimately with its end. Pieter Stuyvesant, then 37, had won his spurs in the West Indies as a soldier in the service of the WIC. He was posted to the colony after commanding the Dutch garrison on the island of Curaçao, a well-known smugglers' den. Renowned for his bravery - he had lost a leg in a fight with the Spanish - he was rewarded for his years of loyal service with the governorship of the disorderly colony on the east coast of North America.

Stuyvesant was a formal and authoritarian but competent administrator who began by introducing strict measures to bring the situation under control. He ordered the closure of a number of taverns and brothels, issued numerous ordinances and announced penalties for law-breaking. Although New Netherland never entirely lost the aura of a frontier society, Stuyvesant succeeded in firmly establishing his authority and restoring the colonists' confidence in the future. In the eighteen years of his governorship New Amsterdam developed from an outpost constantly under threat into a thriving commercial port. Few Indians still remained in the surrounding countryside; the majority had been driven out by the colonists and others had died in the wars or from imported diseases. The lower reaches of the Hudson were securely in the hands of the European newcomers. The greatest threat to the colony was thought to have passed.

While the population of New Netherland had grown, that of the English colonies in whose midst it lay like a wedge had grown faster. Right from the beginning the English had laid claim to the whole of the Atlantic coast of North America and had constantly encroached on the Company's territory. The Dutch being too few to colonize their border areas effectively, English settlers could move in without much difficulty. By the time of Stuyvesant's arrival a substantial part of the original territory, which stretched from Delaware to Cape Cod, had passed into English hands. It was a process which Stuyvesant, hampered by a shortage of new immigrants and an almost total lack of support from the WIC's directors, was powerless to

halt. In 1650 he concluded an agreement with the New Englanders in Hartford, Connecticut (an English settlement in what was still officially Dutch territory), but it was never ratified by London or The Hague.

The fate of New Netherland was finally decided by the rivalry between the two European maritime powers. In 1663 Charles II had generously presented his brother, the Duke of York, with all the land between the Delaware and the Connecticut, blithely disregarding the fact that it belonged to the Dutch. At that moment the two nations were not at war, so the duke could not very well claim his proprietary rights. It was clear, however, that sooner or later the situation would give rise to conflict.

The Second Anglo-Dutch War broke out in 1664, and soon afterwards four English frigates were dispatched to New Netherland. Knowing they were on their way, Stuyvesant appealed for help from his superiors in Amsterdam. It was not forthcoming. The directors insisted there was no need for alarm. The English flagship anchored in Gravesend Bay and her commander, Captain Richard Nicolls, informed

Captain Richard Nicolls informed Stuyvesant: "In His Majestie's name I do demand the towne, situate upon the island commonly known by the name of Manhatoes with all the forts thereunto belonging."

Stuyvesant: "In His Majestie's name I do demand the towne, situate upon the island commonly known by the name of Manhatoes with all the forts thereunto belonging." The situation was hopeless. Stuyvesant had only a small force under his command, the fortifications were in disrepair and the colonists had no appetite for such an unequal battle. His first instinct as a military man was to fight, but he knew that the ultimate result would be the destruction of his life's work. The colony passed into English hands without a shot being fired. Except for a brief interlude in 1673, when the town, since renamed New York, was recaptured during the Third Anglo-Dutch War, this marked the end of the Dutch regime in North America.

The demise of New Netherland also rang the death knell of a colony on the Delaware, an idealistic experiment initiated by Pieter Cornelisz Plockhoy. In his Kort en Klaar Plan (Brief and Clear Plan) he had announced his intention to found a settlement for "the many poor and needy families" in Amsterdam. In this new community everyone would be equal, slavery would not exist, and words like "manservant" and "maidservant" would be taboo. Religious bigotry would not be tolerated, nor would blasphemy and drunkenness. In 1663 Plockhoy and 41 followers left for America to convert his dream into reality. But international politics brought it to a terrible end. The English destroyed the colony and sold its inhabitants into slavery in Virginia.

Back in the Netherlands, Stuyvesant had to account for the loss of the colony, but despite the efforts of the Company's directors to make him the scapegoat he was absolved of all blame. He could not be held accountable in any way for what had happened. Even if he had received the help he needed from the mother country, it is doubtful whether the incorporation of this Dutch enclave into the surrounding English territories could have been postponed for long. Later, the much more extensive French regions in Canada were equally powerless to fend off the same fate.

After his acquittal Stuyvesant returned to the colony where he had lived for almost twenty years, and where his children had been born. Up

Pieter Stuyvesant, stained glass window in St. Mark's church in the Bowery, New York

to his death in 1672 he lived on his bouwerij (farm) in the district still called the Bowery, and was buried in his private chapel. A memorial plate (incidentally giving the wrong date of birth) is to be seen on a wall of St. Mark's Church now occupying the site of the chapel. His ghost, limping on a silver-mounted wooden leg, is said to haunt the ambulatory of the church at night.

A tale of two republics

3

After the loss of New Netherland, Dutch influence in North America was by no means at an end. Indeed, the reverse seemed to be true. For many years New York houses were still built in the Dutch style, with gables, window shutters and raised stoops, even though there was no danger of flooding as in Amsterdam. Not only did most of the original inhabitants remain, but they were joined by a fresh influx of immigrants from the Netherlands. The majority took British nationality in order to be able to continue their trading activities under the Navigation Act, which specified that only English ships could carry goods to and from English ports. The old Dutch commercial families of New Amsterdam became part of the New York ruling classes. New immigrants usually trekked inland to establish farms far beyond the borders of the old colony. In 1683 a group of

Mennonites and Quakers arrived in Pennsylvania, some of whom settled around Philadelphia. The majority were Dutch, but having come from an area near the German border, they were frequently mistaken for Germans, and their main settlement was later named Germantown.

As late as the nineteenth century many New Yorkers of Dutch descent still spoke Dutch at home. Services in the Dutch Reformed Church long continued to be held in the language, in some cases persisting into the twentieth century. After a time the ministers were no longer trained in the Netherlands but in the theology faculty of Rutgers College, the college where many of the sons of old Dutch families were educated.

A good many of the old settlements retained their original Dutch names, most of which were eventually anglicized, like Breukelen (Brooklyn), Haarlem (Harlem) and Vlissingen

Double Dutch

According to what is probably an apocryphal story, Dutch almost became the language of the United States. Early in the War of Independence some radical spirits insisted that English, the language of the royal tyrant across the sea, could not be spoken in the home of the free. They proposed that Dutch, still widely spoken in the states of New York and New Jersey, be adopted as the national language. The proposal was defeated - by one vote, it is said - thus sparing the new republic a lot of bother. Dutch, with its guttural G, is not easy to pronounce (someone once described it as a throat condition rather than a language). Hence the term double Dutch for speech that is incomprehensible. However that may be, Dutch has left its mark on American speech, which has absorbed more words from the early Dutch settlers than from any other non-English speaking migrant group. The majority of them have become such everyday words that no-one thinks about their origin. They are words like boss (from the Dutch baas), cooky (koekje), coleslaw (kool and sla, the Dutch for cabbage and salad), dope (from doop, meaning sauce or gravy), dumb (dom), and golf (kolf, originally a Dutch game). The mighty dollar is the American version of the daalder, an old Dutch coin. Even the word Yankee seems originally to have been used by or of the Dutch, probably as a corruption of the typically Dutch name, Jan Kees.

In addition, the Dutch are represented indirectly in American speech. The English bequeathed to their former colony a number of expressions relating to their greatest trading rivals, none of them flattering: Dutch concert, a confusion of languages or sounds; Dutch courage, the false courage derived from alcohol; a Dutch treat, a treat for which the other has to pay. Place names are another area revealing Dutch influence. East coast localities like Middleburgh, Cape Henlopen (Kaap Hindelopen), Cape May and Block Island (Cornelis May and Adriaen Block were ship's captains in the service of the West India Company), the Schuylkill River and Rensselaerswyck all recall the days of the Dutch colony. New Amsterdam lives on in the names of New York districts such as Manhattan, Staten Island, Yonkers, the Bowery (from bouwerij, the 17th-century Dutch word for farm), Brooklyn (Breukelen), Harlem (Haarlem), Flushing (Vlissingen) and Cramercy (a corruption of Kromme Zee, meaning a winding coastline). Street names going back to that period include Broadway, Beaver Street and Wall Street. The wheel of history seems to have come full circle in Manhattan, for the center of the world economy is located there on the original Walstraat, occupied centuries ago by the Dutch merchants who in their day were the dominant figures in world trade.

They were represented in all social classes and all political groupings. Not surprisingly, therefore, Dutch Americans were to be found on both sides at the time of the Declaration of Independence.

(Flushing). Some localities in New York, New Jersey and Pennsylvania were essentially Dutch for many years. In The Knickerbocker History of New York, published at the beginning of the nineteenth century, Washington Irving poked fun at these clannish Dutch communities in which he had lived for a time.

Despite their tendency to retain their ethnic identity, over the hundred or so years following the capture of New Amsterdam the Dutch put down strong roots in American society. They were represented in all social classes and all political groupings. Not surprisingly, therefore, Dutch Americans were to be found on both sides at the time of the Declaration of Independence. Thousands served in George Washington's army, including John Philip Schuyler, one of his generals, and the influential Dutch Reformed Church was fully behind the Revolution.

But it was not only in the New World that the Dutch became involved in the American War of Independence. While no longer the great power of a century before, the Republic was still an important European state; more particularly, it was an extremely wealthy one. The Continental Congress therefore sought support in Amsterdam for its struggle against Great Britain. In 1780 John Adams, one of the prime movers of the Revolution and a future president of the United States, was sent as an envoy to The Hague to enlist support for the American cause.

Britain had already requested the aid of the Republic in 1775, asking it to send troops (the "Scots Brigade") to America to help defeat the rebels. Stadholder Willem V was willing, but a considerable part of the nation was not. The country was divided into two camps, both of which viewed the American Revolution in its relevance to their own political situation. The stadholder and his party took the side of established authority, the British Crown, on principle. A large section of the population, regarding Britain as their traditional enemy and fired by their opposition to the stadholder's administration, supported the Americans. In particular, the self-styled Patriots, the party which sought to curb the stadholder's powers, applauded the developments on the

List of arms and ammunition in a complaint lodged by the British ambassador concerning Dutch arms supplies to the American rebels

other side of the Atlantic. In the States General, Joan Derk van der Capellen, an ardent advocate of the American cause, argued passionately against dispatching the Scots Brigade because the rebels had right on their side. His eloquence convinced the assembly, and the Republic remained neutral.

In the event, the Americans did get the aid they wanted from the Netherlands, if not always for idealistic reasons. The new state needed arms for the struggle, and Amsterdam was one of the world's principal arms markets. In trade and commerce, the Republic's merchants were both capable and ever alert to the possibility of making a profit. The British were highly incensed by the many Dutch ships running their naval blockade of America. The small Caribbean island of St. Eustatius played a central role in this contraband trade. In 1777 alone, upwards of 2,400 ships were cleared in and out of the island's port. Ships arrived every day in America's eastern seaboard ports, the majority of them carrying gunpowder and weapons. So the salute at St. Eustatius was set in a clearly defined context rendering its

Admiral John Paul Jones "Sketched at the Amsterdam Schouwburg, 9 October 1779"

significance more than symbolic.

Britain watched the activities of the officially non-partisan Dutch with growing displeasure. The smugglers' den known as the Golden Rock in the West Indies, measuring a mere 21 square kilometers, was a particular thorn in her side. Moreover, in 1779 the British were powerless to prevent an American naval ship commanded by John Paul Jones from eluding his pursuers and finding refuge in the waters of Texel, an island off the Dutch coast. Naval heroes, especially those who harried the British, were extremely popular with the Dutch, and Jones was welcomed with great enthusiasm by the local population: "Everything that charity could do ... was already being done by the lovely Holland dames and daughters of the Helder ... Every day these blessed women came to the ships in great numbers ... bringing with them for our wounded all the numberless little comforts of Dutch homes, a tribute that came from the hearts of the people, and therefore far overlaid in effect all statecraft and all diplomacy against us."

For the British this was the last

Britain declares war on the Netherlands, 1780

straw. At the end of 1780 they declared war on the Republic. The Fourth Anglo-Dutch War was a disaster for the Dutch. The contraband trade through St. Eustatius came to an abrupt end in February 1781 when the island was captured by a British fleet. Just what havoc it had wreaked is apparent from a letter written by the British commander, Admiral Rodney, to his superiors in London: "I hope this Island will never be returned to the Dutch; it has been more detrimental to England than all the forces of her enemies, and alone has contributed to the continuance of the American war." The island was eventually returned to the Dutch, but played no further part in the American War of Independence.

John Adams's first impressions of the Republic of the United Provinces verged on the lyrical. It was a country shaped by its inhabitants, who had wrested it from the sea and from a foreign tyrant: "It is like no other. It is all the effect of industry and the work of art." Like many of the American rebels, he regarded the Republic as a model state. After living there for a

John Adams's first impressions of the Republic of the United Provinces verged on the lyrical. It was a country shaped by its inhabitants, who had wrested it from the sea and from a foreign tyrant: "It is like no other. It is all the effect of industry and the work of art."

time, however, he changed this view.

It was not the paragon of openness and freedom he had taken it to be, but a society governed in Byzantine fashion by a wealthy oligarchy. In their negotiations with the American envoy, the Dutch moreover displayed a hard-headedness and lack of idealism that soon subdued the warmth of his feelings. True, they felt great sympathy for the rebels' cause - ironically, the opposition parties regarded America as a model of freedom and virtue - and if there were profits to be made Dutch merchants were willing to go to considerable lengths, but that did not extend to putting their money into risky ventures. The Amsterdam bankers were not prepared to make available the funds so urgently needed for the survival of the new state so long as it was not officially recognized by their own Republic.

Adams then devoted his energies to lobbying for recognition. In his attempts to procure the political and, above all, the financial support of the Republic, he was obliged to steer very carefully between the many rocks and shoals of the political system. The establishment, in which a constant

power struggle was going on between the various factions of the governing class - the regents - and the aristocrats seeking to establish a monarchy was highly complex, undemocratic and opaque. Not for nothing was the Dutch system repeatedly cited by the writers of the American Constitution as a prime example of what to avoid.

In April 1781 Adams, then in Leiden, wrote two memorials, one to the States General and one to the Stadholder, petitioning for their recognition of the United States. Stressing the similarities and historical ties between the two states, he wrote: "If there was ever among nations a natural alliance, one may be formed between two republics." He argued that the Dutch were morally obliged to support the American revolution if they were not to "pass a censure upon the greatest actions of [their] immortal ancestors." In addition, recognition of the United States would bring huge financial rewards: America would quite certainly become an important market for Dutch trade and commerce. An alliance between the two countries was "clearly ordained

John Adams - engraving, 1782
"Envoy of the North-American States to the
United Provinces"

John Adams:

"The standard of the

United States waves and

flies at The Hague

in triumph...

When I go to heaven,

I shall look down

over the battlements

with pleasure upon

the stripes and stars

wantoning in the wind

at The Hague."

by providence."

The negotiations lasted a year, during which it became increasingly evident that the rebels were gaining the upper hand. France, the first country to accord full recognition to the United States, and eager to forge a French-Dutch-American alliance against the British, instructed her representatives in the Republic to bring pressure to bear on the Dutch authorities. On April 19, 1782, the States General recognized the United States as a sovereign nation, making the Republic the second power to do so. In October of that year the two countries signed a treaty of amity and commerce, each according the other the status of most favored nation and providing for eternal peace and friendship between them. The first American embassy abroad was established at The Hague.

The tremendous pressure under which John Adams had lived throughout that time brought him to the brink of paranoia. Towards the end he was obsessed by the idea that he was surrounded by secret agents intent on sabotaging his mission. The redeeming recognition of his country by the States General was his long-awaited moment of glory: "The standard of the United States waves and flies at The Hague in triumph ... When I go to heaven, I shall look down over the battlements with pleasure upon the stripes and stars wantoning in the wind at The Hague."

His second aim, to procure a loan from the Amsterdam bankers, was however not yet achieved. His negotiating partners were much less impressed by the new political situation than he was, and declined to extend unlimited credit to the United States on those grounds alone. The American representatives were distressed by their attitude.

Adams described the Dutch as "worse than the English ... a nation of idolators at the shrine of Mammon." Benjamin Franklin observed that the Republic was "no longer a nation but a great shop; and I begin to think it has no other principle or sentiments but those of a shopkeeper." There may have been some truth in this, but it was also the case that they wanted the Dutch to invest huge sums in an enterprise that was by no means without risk. Their complaints reveal the frustrations of proud founding fathers who felt they were expected to grovel in order to obtain the funds needed for the realization of their great ideals. Adams described his situation as that of "a man in the midst of the ocean, negotiating for his life among a school of sharks." Despite these many difficulties, he accomplished his mission in July 1782, arranging with a group of bankers for a loan of 5 million guilders at 5 percent interest. The loans provided by Dutch bankers formed the backbone of the American economy in the following years. Foreign loans, of which the great majority were raised in the Netherlands, comprised 43 percent of the revenues of the American government between 1788 and 1791, and a good 26 percent up to 1795. The United States issued no further loans after that date, but the Dutch-American financial relationship continued until 1809, when the earlier loans had all been fully paid off.

The Dutch also invested directly in the new country. The Holland Land Company purchased large tracts of land in New York and Pennsylvania, and a substantial part of the United States' purchase of the Louisiana Territory from France was financed by Dutch investors. Dutch funds were invested in infrastructure projects, the establishment of banks, the building of the nation's capital, Washington D.C., and the construction of railroads and canals, including the Erie Canal. Between 1825 and 1840 Dutch financiers provided 90 percent of the funds invested in a variety of canal projects.

Dutch contributions to the American economy diminished somewhat during the nineteenth century. A brief upsurge took place in 1863 with a massive response in the Netherlands to the sale of Union bonds, thus providing the North with vital support in the Civil War. In the second half of the century Dutch investors also provided a large proportion of the capital required for the construction of American railroads, in which some 600 million dollars (roughly one billion today) of Dutch money had been invested by 1906. What made this all the more remarkable was the fact that the same financiers showed little interest in the construction of a railroad network in

The US representative Alexander Hill Everett advised his government to close the mission altogether: "Nothing stirs in the Netherlands."

the Netherlands.

The political significance of the Netherlands to the United States spiraled downwards from the end of the eighteenth century. In 1795 France invaded the Republic and the stadholder fled abroad. The opposition was jubilant, and a new state, the Batavian Republic, was proclaimed. Just as the Americans had studied the Dutch model in founding their state, so the Dutch now looked across the Atlantic for inspiration in framing a new constitution. In the end, however, the constitution was based on that of France, which was to be the dominant influence in the affairs of the Netherlands in the following years.

The American envoy to The Hague witnessed the events in this time of turmoil with disapproval. From the moment of his arrival in 1794, John Quincy Adams, like his father a future president of his country, wrote reports expressing scant sympathy for what was happening in the Netherlands. In his view, it had ceased to be an independent, influential power in Europe, and was now completely overshadowed by Britain and still

more by France. After his return to America in 1797, The Hague sank to the status of a backwater post for American diplomats. Between 1801 and 1815 there was no American envoy at all, and in 1819 - the Netherlands had meanwhile become a monarchy - the US representative Alexander Hill Everett advised his government to close the mission altogether: "Nothing stirs in the Netherlands." Fortunately his advice was not followed.

Dutch presidents

Of the forty-two presidents of the United States since 1789, three were of Dutch extraction: Martin Van Buren (1782-1862), Theodore Roosevelt (1858-1919) and Franklin D. Roosevelt (1882-1945).

Martin Van Buren was born in Old Kinderhook, one of the enclaves in New York which had kept their Dutch identity. Time seemed to have stood still in Old Kinderhook: a century and a half after the territory had become an English colony the language of the inhabitants was still Dutch. They were practically all interrelated. It was there that Washington Irving. who lived there for a few months, created the character of Rip Van Winkle.

The young Martin, red-headed and short of stature, grew up in the tavern kept by his father, where the eleven members of the family and six slaves lived crowded together above the taproom. He qualified as a lawyer and became involved in politics, for which he displayed an exceptional talent. Through his professionalism and guile he rose to the top of the recently formed Democratic Party, but those qualities also earned him a mixed reputation and nicknames like "the red fox" and "the little magician". Van Buren was one of the architects of the "spoils system" enabling a newly elected president to make his own appointments to official posts. His critics accused him of lowering American politics to the level of an unsavoury power game.

His contemporaries either praised him lavishly or reviled him wholeheartedly, but even his greatest rivals could not deny that he was capable, honest and courageous.

After some years in the Senate, Van Buren was elected governor of New York. His incumbency was brief, for forty-three days later he was summoned to Washington to be President Jackson's Secretary of State. Eight years after that, in 1837, he succeeded Jackson as president. His presidency should have been the crowning achievement of his political career, but unfortunately for him, the country was hard hit by an economic crisis during his administration, and he was forced to leave the White House in 1841 after sustaining a shattering electoral defeat at the hands of William Harrison. Although he was proud of his Dutch heritage (the first Van Buren had arrived in New Netherland in 1633), it played little part in Van Buren's political career. Despite their clannish tendencies, Dutch Americans were deeply divided politically and never formed a single block of voters supporting their own candidate. His background was of importance to him only in his personal life. In the Netherlands in 1853, he visited the village of Buren in the hope of tracing his ancestors. He met people of the same name, with whom he conversed in the Dutch he had learned in Old Kinderhook, but failed to find any lead to his own origins. Like many other Dutch Americans, he found that time had irrevocably buried the past.

Theodore Roosevelt (president from 1901 to 1909) and Franklin D. Roosevelt (president from 1933 until his death in 1945) also belonged to a family going back to the time of New Netherland. Claes Martensen van Roosevelt bought a 48-acre farm in New Amsterdam in 1644. Theodore Roosevelt wrote in his autobiography: "From that time for the next seven generations from father to son every one of us was born on Manhattan Island." However, as not all of them married women of Dutch ancestry in those two

Princess Juliana, future Queen of The Netherlands, visiting President Franklin D. Roosevelt and his wife Eleanor Roosevelt, Hyde Park

hundred or more years, the Roosevelts were not of exclusively Dutch descent. The two presidents were nonetheless proud of their Dutch name. In his second year at Harvard, Franklin wrote a paper on "The Roosevelt family in New Amsterdam before the Revolution". Later, wishing to know more about his forebears, he employed researchers to find out where Claes Roosevelt had come from. The trail led to the village of Oud-Vossemeer on Tholen, an island in the southwestern province of Zeeland.

In the 1920s Franklin Roosevelt was active in the Netherlands-America Foundation, aimed at promoting good relations between the two countries. As a member of the Holland Society, one of his interests was the study of Dutch colonial architecture in New York. In 1935, on the fiftieth anniversary of the Society, he observed: "The influence of New Netherland on the whole Colonial period of our history, which culminated in the War for Independence, has not as yet been fully recognized ... It is an influence which manifests itself today in almost every part of our Union of States." Theodore Roosevelt visited the Netherlands in 1910, shortly after his second term as president. He was pleasantly surprised by the warmth of his welcome: "Late in the evening we crossed into Holland, and at the first place we stopped there was a wildly enthusiastic mob of ten thousand people cheering and calling." Roosevelt was particularly impressed by the way in which the Dutch in the nineteenth century had recovered from their loss of world power status and the economic decline that followed. He was less enchanted with Queen Wilhelmina, whom he found much too imperious for the ruler of such a miniature country.

Franklin Roosevelt, on the other hand, who took the oath on his old Dutch family bible at his inauguration, had a much better relationship with Wilhelmina. As an exile from her country during World War II, she visited him at Hyde Park with her daughter Juliana, and he was godfather to one of her grandchildren. She recorded in her memoirs how Roosevelt took her to the train after one such visit in the summer of 1943: "I can still see him waving to me from his car as the train moved out. His last words contained good wishes for the resurrection of the Netherlands which held such a special place in his heart and for us all."

The Amsterdam II, an immigrant ship belonging to the Holland-America Line, painted by J.H. Wijsmuller, c. 1890

Velvet coats and wooden shoes

4

*Few people emigrated:
the 250,000 who went
to America comprised
90 percent of all Dutch
men and women who
left to settle elsewhere.*

The Dutch part in the mass migration of Europeans to America in the nineteenth and twentieth centuries was a modest one. Between 1820 and 1920, 250,000 migrants left the Netherlands for the New World, a negligible number compared to the millions of Germans, Irish, Italians and Russians who left their homes in the same period. This stemmed partly from the limited size of the Dutch population, but it may also be said that, taken as a whole, few people emigrated: the 250,000 who went to America comprised 90 percent of all Dutch men and women who left to settle elsewhere.

The Dutch migrants displayed a number of specific characteristics. The majority were farmers who saw greater opportunities in America. By and large, they came from one or two particular localities where the soil was usually of poor quality; in their new homeland they clustered together in typically Dutch communities.

Many of these farmers migrated for religious as well as economic reasons. One of the factors precipitating the revolt against Spain had been the demand for religious freedom, and religious conflicts were still not a thing of the past. Throughout the centuries the Dutch faithful were remarkable for their schismatic tendencies, giving rise to a multiplicity of churches and sects which to outsiders were often barely distinguishable one from the other. Such a schism occurred in the official Dutch Reformed Church in 1834. The seceders, in whose eyes the doctrine of the state church was not strict enough, founded the Protestant Reformed Church. It was not accorded recognition by the state and its members, many of whom were farmers in the poorer rural areas, were long regarded as second-class citizens.

Of Dutch descent

The majority of Dutch people who contributed to the development of American society did so in anonymity as industrial workers and farmers. Yet there were also those who made a more uniquely personal contribution to American culture. Some were recent immigrants; others were descendants of earlier settlers. There is no means of telling to what extent their success was due to their Dutch background. But it was certainly a factor of which many of them were proud. Cornelius Vanderbilt, a nineteenth-century farmer's son, built one of the greatest fortunes in the United States. His family had settled in America 150 years before. Nor was he alone in achieving such success: John van Heusen, a manufacturer of shirts and collars, expanded his business into a multi-million dollar enterprise; Walter P. Chrysler founded the motor company which bears his name; John Dykstra rose to be president of General Motors and, from 1961 onwards, the Ford Motor Company.

The forefathers of twentieth-century personalities like Humphrey Bogart, film director Cecil B. De Mille and journalist Walter Cronkite emigrated from the Netherlands to America at the time of New Netherland. Audrey Hepburn spent her youth in the Netherlands. Great writers such as Walt Whitman and Herman Melville were also of Dutch descent.

Science is represented by the pediatrician Benjamin Spock, William Kolff, the inventor of the artificial kidney, and Robert J. Van de Graaf, physicist and inventor of the electrostatic generator which bears his name.

The armed services include General James A. Van Fleet, commander of the UN armed forces in Korea from 1951 to 1953, Alexander A. Vandergrift, commander of the Marine Corps from 1944 to 1947, and Hoyt S. Vandenberg, USAF Chief of Staff from 1948 to 1953.

The list would not be complete without the arts. The long and glorious tradition of painting in the Netherlands features names like Rembrandt, Vermeer and Van Gogh. In the twentieth century, a number of major

Audrey Hepburn

Morning: the springs, 1983, by Willem de Kooning (1904-1997)

Dutch artists worked for some years in the United States, taking part in American life and influencing American culture in return. Both Piet Mondrian and, later, Karel Appel worked in New York. Willem De Kooning went to America in 1926 at the age of 22, working at first as a house painter. He was eventually recognized as one of the most important American abstract expressionists of the twentieth century.

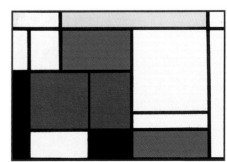

A composition by Piet Mondrian (1872-1944)

Burdened by these economic and religious problems, some decided to try their luck elsewhere.

The first group of religious migrants arrived in New York in 1846. Led by their minister, Van Raalte, they moved soon afterwards to the Midwest, where they found a suitable site for a settlement in Michigan. Shortly thereafter they were joined by new waves of immigrants, so that before long the region between Lake Michigan and Grand Rapids was almost entirely populated by Dutch settlers and became known as de Kolonie. The main settlement was named Holland, while the names of others in the vicinity recalled the regions or in some cases the villages from which the settlers had come: Harlem, Zutphen, Zeeland, Overisel. Another migrant group founded the colony of Pella, in Iowa, named after the place where according to tradition the early Christians found refuge after the destruction of Jerusalem.

Religious groups did not constitute the majority of Dutch immigrants. Their numbers were certainly appreciable, amounting to some

28 percent altogether, a remarkable figure given the fact that they comprised no more than 1.7 percent of the total Dutch population, but group migration was also a frequent phenomenon in other contexts. For instance, various families from one village often migrated together. In the period from 1820 to 1880 three quarters of all Dutch immigrants came from only 134 localities, most of them in the less fertile rural areas. As a consequence of the fact that so many had emigrated and settled together, the new Dutch Americans, like their predecessors a century before, integrated much less rapidly than other nationalities into the mainstream of American society. In 1850, 72 percent lived in only 16 counties, principally in Michigan, Iowa and Wisconsin.

The tendency to cluster together was most marked among orthodox Calvinist immigrants. The Dutch in the Midwest clung to many of their old customs. Visiting the newly-founded Pella in 1847, an American journalist was astonished to find "...a new race of beings ... a broad-shouldered race in velvet coats and wooden shoes..." In their new homeland, most of them continued to live as before. Market gardens were begun near urban centers, in many cases after waterlogged subsoil which had defeated the attempts of others had been drained by traditional Dutch methods. Mixed farms and dairy farms, another Dutch specialty, appeared on the plains, and a few bulb-growers resumed their former occupation. Up to the 1920s a conspicuously large number of Americans of Dutch descent were active in the agricultural sector, amounting in fact to twice their proportion of the total population.

The religious peculiarities of the Dutch were likewise transplanted to their new surroundings as part of everyday life. An American resident of Holland, Michigan, remarked that his fellow villagers, for whom religion had been a reason for emigrating, behaved with a surprising lack of piety in church, not bothering to remove their hats and beginning to fill their pipes before the end of the service. But they had certainly brought with them their finely honed aptitude for theological hair-splitting. True to form, within ten years a typically Dutch schism appeared in the traditional Reformed Protestant Dutch Church, to which the majority of the immigrants belonged. The seceders founded the True Dutch Reformed Church, renamed in 1890 the Christian Reformed Church; unlike the rival congregation they continued to conduct their services in Dutch, and forbade insurance and women's votes.

The Dutch communities were not fully assimilated into American society until the time of the Civil War. The second-generation sons who volunteered for service, generally in the Union army, became better acquainted with their compatriots and discovered that they themselves were first and foremost Americans. Also, during the war years the flow of Dutch immigrants came to a halt. Returning home, the soldiers helped to Americanize their communities, which at that time also began to disperse westwards, founding sister colonies in the Midwest - Iowa (Sioux County), Minnesota (Prinsburg, Holland) the Dakotas - and later in Montana (Manhattan), Washington (Lynden),

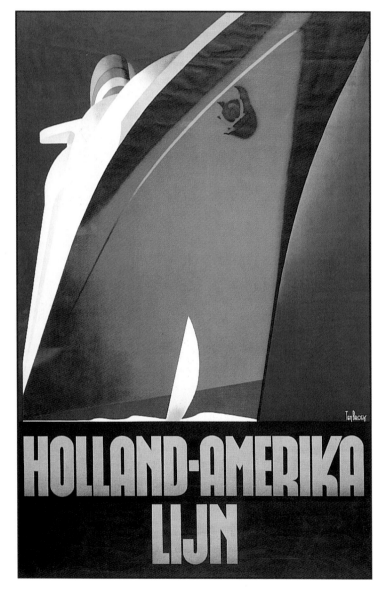

HOLLAND-AMERIKA LIJN

Utah and California (Hynes). The inhabitants of the new towns and villages were both newcomers from the Netherlands - 175,000 more arrived between the end of the Civil War and 1910 - and descendants of earlier immigrants. For most of them the first years were a struggle for survival. The average sum brought to America by Dutch immigrants was a mere 30 dollars. Hendrik van der Pol, who trekked to Dakota in 1885, owned only a wagonload of furniture, a cow and a horse to pull the wagon. The first dwellings in Dakota were usually huts made of turf (called Dakota bricks), and the settlers had to contend with droughts, swarms of locusts, blizzards and isolation. It was not unusual for six months to pass without their seeing anyone but their families.

As before, the Dutch tended to settle together in close-knit groups, some of which expanded into thriving communities. Though they eventually became fully Americanized - a process

Poster by Wim ten Broek, 1936
Holland-America Line

accelerated, as with the Civil War earlier, by the First World War - Dutch influence is still marked, if only by the many Dutch names in telephone directories.

After the First World War migration to the United States got under way again, but very slowly. Notwithstanding its neutrality, the Netherlands had suffered from the war: the shipping industry, a vital sector of the economy, had been brought to a virtual standstill by the British naval blockade, and thousands of refugees had fled into the country from Belgium. Immigration quotas introduced by the United States in 1920 reduced the number of potential Dutch immigrants, whose quota was fixed on the basis of their relatively small proportion of the American population. Interest nevertheless remained high, especially after the Second World War. In 1952 there was a waiting list of 40,000 hoping to try their luck in America, of whom only 3,100 could be admitted annually under the quota system. Others had to switch their preference for the United States to other countries, so that only

20 percent of the approximately one million people who left the Netherlands in the post-war years ended up in the United States.

Dutch nationals from the former Dutch East Indies were a separate category. In the decade from 1953 to 1963 some 35,000 emigrated to America. Many of them were of mixed Dutch-Indonesian parentage and as such had occupied a separate place in colonial society. When Dutch rule came to an end with the proclamation of Indonesia's independence in 1949, 300,000 moved to the Netherlands. They found it difficult to adapt to a cold, wet, overpopulated country which was still recovering from the war years, and which to many of them was new and strange. Special laws providing for the admission of refugees passed by Congress in the late 1950s enabled some to go to the United States. The majority settled in southern California, where they assimilated so quickly that they were soon regarded as a highly successful group of immigrants. Within the space of one generation they became integrated into American society.

Poster by Wim ten Broek, 1938 – Visit the New York World's Fair with the Holland-America Line

NEW YORK

WERELDTENTOONSTELLING

EXCURSIES PER

HOLLAND-AMERIKA LIJN

If their share of migration was a modest one in terms of numbers, the Dutch were closely associated with the flow of immigration in another way. Beginning in 1871, steamships maintained a regular service between Rotterdam, the major Dutch seaport, and New York. In the first 25 years of the Nederlandsch-Amerikaansche Stoomvaart-Maatschappij, better known as the Holland-America Line (HAL), its ships carried 130,000 emigrants from all parts of Europe to the New World.

The HAL, which Americans also called "the spotless fleet", was a well-oiled emigration machine. Emigrants who booked a passage in Eastern Europe went to Leipzig, in Germany, and were accommodated in the company's hotel before boarding special trains which took them to Rotterdam. There they were met by HAL representatives, who spoke Polish, Russian and German, and escorted to the Rotterdam "emigrants hotel", to ensure that people awaiting their sailing date were not obliged to stay in small, grimy hotels, the shipping company had built a 400-bed hotel. While there they were given a medical examination to detect diseases that could block their admission to the United States, it being after all in the company's interest to keep the flow of immigrants going. For thousands of future Americans, the company hotel on the Wilhelminakade was the last stop on their journey from the old continent to Hoboken, New Jersey - the other side of "the floating bridge" spanning the Atlantic - where they first set foot in their new fatherland.

Dining room in the Holland-America Line's hotel for emigrants, 1920

Apart from passengers, the HAL carried 5 million tons of goods across the Atlantic in that period. The US economy was fast expanding, and the Dutch economy was recovering from a long spell of stagnation. Handling goods in transit to the industrialized German hinterland, the Netherlands regained its former status of a trading nation. It also exported agricultural products such as dairy produce, plants, flower bulbs and spices, and Dutch East Indies products like sugar, tobacco and rubber, which accounted for a substantial part of exports to the United States.

Between 1870 and 1900 the value of exports from the Netherlands and its colonies to the United States rose from 1.3 to 44.8 million dollars, and of imports from 6.4 to 89.4 million dollars. Over the next few years sugar exports were brought to a virtual standstill by high US tariffs. Yet in 1913 exports to the United States still amounted to 38.2 million dollars, against imports of 125.9 million. With this volume of trade, the Netherlands, with a population of less than 10 million and one of the smallest countries in Europe, was fourth on the

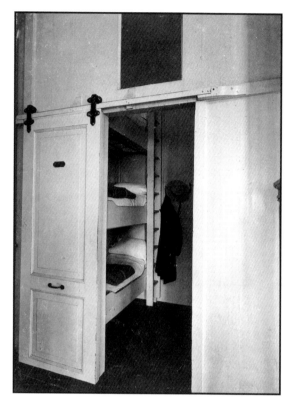

Bedroom in the Holland-America Line's hotel for emigrants, 1920

mid-1930s. Between 1935 and 1940 more than 230 million dollars in Dutch capital were invested in the United States; in the same period Dutch assets in US banks grew by 168 million dollars. In August 1939 Dutch investments totaled 860 million dollars, making the Netherlands the third biggest foreign investor in the USA after Great Britain and Canada.

Dutch confidence in American trade and commerce remained high. After the Second World War investments increased still further. With a share of 22.5 percent, the Netherlands was the major foreign investor in the United States in 1981. In 1987 total Dutch investments amounted to 47 billion dollars, 11 billion less than Britain but a good 5 billion ahead of Japanese investments. In that year Dutch companies provided employment for more than 250,000 Americans.

If economic relations between the two countries have shown a steady upward trend throughout the present century, political relations have been subject to more fluctuation without, however, the emergence of serious conflict.

Before the Netherlands became

list of the United States' European trading partners.

Transatlantic commerce was not restricted to goods; capital likewise crossed the ocean. After the nineteenth-century boom Dutch investors tended to hold back during the first decades of the twentieth century, but regained confidence in the involved in the war in 1940, President Roosevelt, himself a member of one of the oldest New York families of Dutch descent, invited Queen Wilhelmina and her family to come to America if they were forced to seek refuge abroad. After the German invasion the Queen and Princess Juliana and her children, of whom the eldest is now Queen Beatrix, visited the president several times at his country residence, Hyde Park. He was deeply concerned with the fate of the small country from which his ancestors had come centuries before. Three weeks before he died, when part of the Netherlands had been liberated by Allied troops including 110,000 Americans, he wrote to Wilhelmina, "You can be very certain I shall not forget the country of my origin."

In 1947 the Dutch became involved in armed conflict in order to reimpose their authority in Indonesia, which had declared its independence from the Netherlands in 1945, invoking the hallowed principle of the unalienable right to life, liberty and the pursuit of happiness. Having received American support in its unsuccessful effort to repulse the Japanese attack on the colony in 1942, the Netherlands assumed that the United States would now back its campaign to recover the colony. During the war years President Roosevelt's standpoint had been that the Netherlands, unlike France, should regain control of its colonies in Southeast Asia. After some hesitation, however, the American government sided with the Indonesian republicans. This came as a shock to the Dutch government, which realized too late that the political climate had changed, leaving it no option but to withdraw its troops and end the war. The sovereign Republic of the United States of Indonesia was formally proclaimed in 1949.

A similar situation occurred in the early 1960s. The Netherlands still possessed one colony in Southeast Asia: Western New Guinea, adjacent to Indonesia. Indonesia, which under President Sukarno had constantly laid claim to the colony, threatened in 1961 to take it by force. The United States intervened once again. President Kennedy was exasperated by the attitudes of both Sukarno and the Dutch Foreign Minister, Joseph Luns,

Dutch newspapers on Marshall Aid, October 1948
"Celebrations to welcome Marshall coal"
"The nation's gratitude. Marshall Aid: grist to the economy's mill"
"2/3 of Americans for Marshall Plan. Europe able to pay its own way in 4 years"
"The Netherlands receives the most Marshall Aid per head"
" W.A. Harriman explained ..."
"C.G. Marshall proposed .... "

Each of these two issues caused a temporary chill between the Netherlands and the United States, but had no lasting effect on their overall good relations. The Netherlands owed much of the success of its post-war reconstruction to America's Marshall Aid, of which it was one of the principal beneficiaries. Relations between the two countries were strengthened in other ways as well. Within NATO and in international politics in general the Netherlands became one of America's most faithful allies. In the Korean War Dutch and American troops fought side by side under the flag of the United Nations. More recently, Dutch military units have taken part in the Gulf War and in peace-keeping operations in the former Yugoslavia.

but feared that a crisis in Southeast Asia could drive Sukarno into the arms of the Soviet Union, which was potentially more dangerous than an angry ally in Europe. Thus the United States again aligned itself on the side of Indonesia. In October 1962 the Netherlands transferred the sovereignty of New Guinea to the United Nations; it was annexed by Indonesia a year later.

In the early 1980s the alliance seemed threatened with friction as a result of mass demonstrations in Amsterdam and elsewhere against the deployment on Dutch soil of cruise missiles with nuclear warheads (for that matter, American nuclear weapons had been stationed in the Netherlands since 1957). The European peace movement, which

Hats off to Marshall

Along with other European countries, the Netherlands emerged from the Second World War with its economy shattered. The fighting had brought widespread devastation: dikes were breached, farmlands were inundated, houses lay in ruins. In addition, industrial machinery, rolling stock and other vehicles had been taken to Germany by the occupying forces. The huge investments needed to get the economy moving again were far beyond the capacities of a country so impoverished. Coming as it did after the hardships of the war years, this period of "austerity and constraint" disappointed many hopes and expectations. During the early post-war years recovery was very slow, not just in the Netherlands but in the whole of Europe. The United States Government, and notably

Secretary of State George C. Marshall, realized that the situation and the feelings of frustration it engendered could be exploited by the Soviet Union to enlarge its sphere of influence in Europe. In an address at Harvard University on 5 June 1947, Marshall outlined his

plan for financial assistance to European countries. He attached the condition that the Europeans themselves were to draft a feasible joint program for economic recovery. The Netherlands, as did the majority of West European nations, welcomed the plan and was from the outset a member of the Organization for European Economic Cooperation, the intergovernmental organization set up to administer the recovery

program, which was the forerunner of the Organization for Economic Cooperation and Development (OECD). The US Government sent representatives to Europe for consultation on how the funds could best be used. Everywhere they went, they were welcomed with lavish hospitality; arriving after some delay in the Netherlands, they were given tea and cookies by the socialist prime minister,

Marshall addressing European trade union leaders in Paris

Willem Drees, in his terraced home in The Hague. Some of his officials feared such a reception so lacking in ceremony would have a chilling effect on the high-ranking American diplomats. But in the event the opposite was the case. Averell Harriman, who led the delegation, was deeply impressed. In his view, a country whose prime minister set so little store by the outward trappings of office would put America's economic assistance to the right use.

The first ship carrying goods purchased with Marshall Aid arrived in the Netherlands on April 26, 1948. From then until 1952 the country received upwards of one billion dollars worth of goods, primarily for the food, textile and aviation industries. The Program also enabled the Dutch Government to improve the infrastructure, repair damaged factories and reclaim land in the former Zuyder Zee. Furthermore, more than 1,200 representatives of Dutch agriculture and industry were able to go to the United States to be brought up to date on the latest developments in their sectors. Whereas nearly two centuries earlier Dutch funds had sustained the growth of the United States, the situation was now reversed, with American funds providing a stimulus to the reconstruction of the Netherlands. Alan Valentine and Clarance E. Hunter, the representatives in the Netherlands of the Economic Cooperation Administration, the American body which supervised the implementation of the Program, occupied a uniquely influential position. As representatives of a foreign power, they were involved in virtually every aspect of Dutch economic, monetary and social policy, all of which were normally the exclusive province of national governments. This altogether unique relationship between sovereign states could easily have given rise to tension, but on the whole it worked well. Through nation-wide

Bakery with poster: "More than half your daily bread is baked from Marshall flour"

press and radio campaigns (using slogans like "Hats off to Marshall and coats off for work") the Dutch public was urged to seize this opportunity for economic recovery. And that is precisely what they did, with the result that now, five decades later, the Dutch economy is one of the strongest in Western Europe.

President Bush has his family tree explained to him. Also present: Mrs Barbara Bush, Queen Beatrix, and Prime Minister Lubbers, Leiden 1989

appeared to be centered in the Netherlands, soon came to be known in the United States as "Hollanditis". Opinion polls nevertheless showed that 75 percent of the Dutch population supported membership of NATO, and almost as many declared themselves to be pro-American. Shortly afterwards, the whole issue of Hollanditis faded away.

An incumbent president of the United States came to the Netherlands for the first time in 1989 and was warmly welcomed by the population. One of the places visited by President Bush was Leiden, the town from which one of his forefathers had set out for America with the Pilgrim Fathers. It was 380 years after Henry Hudson sailed the Halve Maen up the river which bears his name, 368 years after the departure of the Pilgrim Fathers, 213 years after the salute at St. Eustatius, and 207 years after the Republic of the United Provinces recognized the United States of America. Throughout those centuries numerous other bonds, economic, cultural and personal, were forged between the two nations. There were intervals of little communication and moments of friction, but there was never a time without contact at all.

Perhaps the simplest and best description of the relationship between the Netherlands and the United States was given by President Bush in St. Peter's Church (Pieterskerk) in Leiden, close by the spot where the Pilgrims once lived: "The Netherlands is an old friend of the United States."

Description of the West Indies by Johannes de Laet:
"Second edition: improved in numerous places, enlarged,
with new maps, ornamented with illustrations of divers
plants and animals"

A story of friendship and misunderstanding

As the Dutch historian J.W. Schulte Nordholt wrote, the history of each country's perception of the other is a story of more than 300 years of "friendship and misunderstanding". Through the centuries the Dutch and Americans have held many exaggerated ideas about the other country, and were disappointed when they proved to bear no resemblance to reality. It started with the stories which circulated in the Republic about the territory around the Hudson River where the West India Company was attempting to found a colony. If the first travelers' tales, reflecting an understandable lack of knowledge, were of no real consequence - like Johannes de Laet's Nieuwe Wereldt, portraying the climate as "mild" and the flora as similar to that of Africa - the flights of fancy of later writers were sometimes totally misleading. As the WIC's need for colonists grew, so too the sun shone ever brighter and the vegetation was ever more luxuriant. By about 1660 New Netherland had been transformed into a land of milk and honey with a climate that could easily withstand comparison with the Caribbean. It was all to no avail, however, because it failed to produce mass migration to the colony. When the Dutch had long gone from the scene and the American colonies were asserting their independence from Britain, many of the revolutionaries looked for inspiration to the war of independence fought by the Dutch against the Spaniards two centuries earlier. The Republic on the North Sea, governed by free burghers, was seen as a model, admittedly far distant in time and place, but all the more inspiring for that. Disillusionment followed for those who discovered that this mythical land of the free was in reality a class society governed by a patrician oligarchy. John Adams, the first American envoy to the Netherlands, observed not long after his arrival: "This country is indeed in a melancholy situation, sunk in ease, devoted to the pursuit of gain, incumbered with a complicated and perplexed constitution, divided among themselves in interest and sentiment, they seem afraid of everything."

Conversely, the many Dutchmen who were likewise aware of these shortcomings saw the American revolution as a beacon lighting the way to the freedom and equality so dismally lacking under the stadholders' administration. America was the symbol of a new beginning, a shining example to the middle classes in their struggle with the regents. François Adriaan van der Kemp, a Leiden clergyman who was a friend of Adams, wrote: "In America the sun of salvation has risen which will also shine upon us." Van der Kemp eventually went to America himself, where he continued his friendship with Adams.

Not much later the great days of the Republic were truly a thing of the past, giving Americans little reason for blind admiration. But their new image of the Netherlands was no less unrealistic than the one it replaced. Instead of a land wrested from the sea, a great nation of freedom fighters, it was transformed in the nineteenth century into a quaint miniature kingdom of wooden shoes, tulips, cheese and windmills. The heroic deeds of the Dutch underwent the same drastic modification: the intrepid opponents of tyranny made way for the village boy with his finger in the dike.

During those years the young, vigorous country across the Atlantic still drew admiring comment in the Netherlands. E.J. Potgieter, one of the sharpest critics of the comatose state of Dutch society in the first half of the nineteenth century, wrote: "America, a haven for every refugee ... offering balm for all wounds ... fulfilment of every need ... bringing together the free and full development of all that is human, what a magnificent prospect you offer; what does the world not still expect of you!"

At the same time, for many conservatives in the Netherlands American culture signified a kind of superficial barbarism devoted exclusively to the satisfaction of material needs and led by vulgar populists. These representatives of the regent class could find nothing praiseworthy in the American democratic experiment.

So incredibly small as the Netherlands was to American visitors, so inconceivably vast was America to Dutch travelers. A correspondent covering the festivities marking the first centennial of the United States in 1876 for the august Nieuwe Rotterdamsche Courant - the first correspondent the paper ever sent to America - was struck with awe by its sheer immensity: "America is a land of the gigantic, of the immeasurable." He was among the first to attempt to correct the image of the United States as a nation without culture or history.

The twentieth century provides further instances of ideological projection. For some Dutch intellectuals, America remained a country of "chaos and superficiality, sentimentality and journalism," a vulgar and materialistic society. But after two world wars had made it only too clear that Europe, for all its pretensions, was itself still mired in barbarism, there were few left holding that opinion. For many America had become more than a country; more than a liberator and the most powerful nation on earth, it represented the future. America's science, technology and way of life were now the ideal, and it could only be a matter of time before those admirable attributes were adopted in Europe.

The dream was shattered in the late 1960s by the Vietnam War, race riots in American cities and the murder of Robert Kennedy and Martin Luther King. The pendulum swung back, and the progressive intellectuals who before had sung America's praises now went to the other extreme of unadulterated anti-Americanism. Although that too faded in time, issues such as crime and the gap between rich and poor can still elicit dire warnings against the danger of becoming "like America."

By and large, however, the tendency to project one's own ideas onto the United States seems to have lessened. Wider travel opportunities and modern communication media have allowed the Dutch to become better acquainted with American reality, and the changed international situation has diminished the need to focus exclusively on one particular country. For most Dutch people the United States is once more a country rather than a symbol. This new perception may give rise to less spectacular ideas, but it is also less likely to lead to disappointment and allows more scope for the fascinating true picture.

Page	Acknowledgements
4,6,8)	Nederlands Scheepvaartmuseum, Amsterdam
10)	National Archives, The Hague
12)	Nederlands Scheepvaartmuseum, Amsterdam
13)	Amsterdam Municipal Archives
14)	Ministry of Foreign Affairs
16,17)	Leiden Municipal Archives
18)	Paulus Swaen Old Maps, Geldrop
21)	Nederlands Scheepvaartmuseum, Amsterdam
24)	National Archives, The Hague
30)	Jan Dorresteijn
34)	National Archives, The Hague
35)	Iconographic Bureau, The Hague
36,38)	National Archives, The Hague
43)	Roosevelt Study Centre, Middelburg
44)	Nederlands Scheepvaartmuseum, Amsterdam
46)	Dutch Theatre Institute; Ministry of Foreign Affairs; Willem de Kooning Revocable Trust / Artists Rights Society, New York / Stedelijk Museum, Amsterdam
49,51)	Maritiem Museum "Prins Hendrik", Rotterdam
52,53)	Rotterdam Municipal Archives
55,56,57)	National Archives, The Hague
58)	R.J.F. van Gulick
60)	University of Amsterdam Library

Bibliography

L. Akveld, *Magnifiek maritiem* (Amsterdam 1992)

W. Bradford, *Of Plymouth Plantation* (New York 1976)

W. Ph. Coolhaas, *A critical survey of studies on Dutch colonial history* (Leiden 1980)

G. F. DeJong, *The Dutch in America* (Boston 1975)

H.W. Van den Doel, P.C. Emmer, H.Ph. Vogel, *Nederland en de Nieuwe Wereld* (Utrecht 1992)

F. Edler, *The Dutch Republic and the American Revolution* (Baltimore 1911)

A. Galema, *Van de ene naar de andere kant* (Groningen 1993)

J. Van Hinte, *Nederlanders in Amerika* (Groningen 1928)

J.A. Jacobs, *De scheepvaart en de handel van de Nederlandse Republiek op Nieuw-Nederland* (Leiden 1989)

J. Jansen van Galen, *Ons laatste oorlogje* (Weesp 1984)

M. Kammen, *Colonial New York* (New York 1975)

R. Kroes, H.O. Neuschäfer (eds.), *The Dutch in North America* (Amsterdam 1991)

A. Lammers, *Uncle Sam en Jan Salie. Hoe Nederland Amerika ontdekte* (Amsterdam 1989)

H.M. Hirschfeld e.a., *Herwonnen Welvaart. De betekenis van het Marshallplan en de Europese Samenwerking* (Den Haag 1954)

G.H. Ligterink, *De Landverhuizers* (Doetinchem 1981)

H.S. Lucas, *Netherlanders in America* (Grand Rapids 1989)

H.S. Lucas, *Dutch immigrant memoirs and related writings* (Assen 1955)

J. Niven, *Martin Van Buren* (New York and Oxford 1978)

J. Presser, *Amerika, van kolonie tot wereldmacht* (Amsterdam 1965)

O.A. Rink, *Holland on the Hudson* (Ithaca 1986)

D. Roos, *Zeeuwen en de Westindische Compagnie* (Hulst 1992)

W.H. Salzmann, *Bedrijfsleven, overheid en handelsbevordering* (Leiden 1994)

J.W. Schulte Nordholt, Robert P. Swieringa (eds.), *A bilateral bicentennial* (Amsterdam 1982)

J.W. Schulte Nordholt, *Triomf en tragiek van de vrijheid* (Amsterdam 1985)

J.W. Schulte Nordholt (ed.), *Two hundred years of Netherlands-American Interaction* (Bryn Mawr 1985)

B. Solow (ed.), *Slavery and the rise of the Atlantic system* (Cambridge 1991)

R. Spruit, *Zout en slaven: de geschiedenis van de Westindische Compagnie* (Houten 1988)

P.R.D. Stokvis, *De Nederlandse trek naar Amerika* (Leiden 1977)

B. Tuchman, *The First Salute* (New York, 1988)

H. en B. Van der Zee, *A sweet and alien land* (New York 1978)

C. Zevenbergen, *Toen zij uit Rotterdam vertrokken* (Zwolle 1990)

Keesings Historisch Archief, vols. 1948 and 1962, *The Leyden Pilgrim Fathers Society, Memories of the Pilgrim Fathers in Holland* (Leiden 1923)